MW00874443

EMERALD

COMPANION

SUHAIB RUMI

Contents

FALL

A heart so heavy
Louder than a drum
Is madness to many
And poetry to some

"I have many sad stories"
said the madman.
"But are you here to put out
my fire, or warm yourselves
as you watch me burn?"

So the people responded,
as they gathered around.
And the winter night
felt cold no more.

She cries in the rain
and storms into the hurricane.
All that trouble to mask her pain
in the madness of seeming sane.

Among the questions that haunt us;
are should I give up and let go,
or hold on and not give up.
And is it giving up to let go,
or is it so if I hold on?

All the pain of destined separation
are shadows cast from a joyous past.
And no sadness is ever felt
without carving space
for even more happiness to fill.
Such is the journey and cycle of life.
A subtle expansion of the universe within.
Like the ever growing cosmos without.

Gracious are the hosts
to joy and comfort
who have never been
strangers to pain.

I fear that if I tell you what
you mean to me, you might be
tempted to use it against me.
So I keep it a secret. Between
myself and the keeper of secrets.
As I take comfort in my prayers
for you, that you'll never know.
There's a madman who cares for
you, more than you'll ever know.

The space where lovers
meet and separate becomes
the birthplace of poetry.

"...*So what went wrong?*"
I began to look elsewhere
for what I had all along.

———————————————

Just because the moon isn't full, doesn't
mean it's incomplete. And so you may not
feel like your true self every day or night,
as you partially glow, and that's quite alright.
For it is due to these contrasting phases that
your fullness is appreciated. No one ever
says "look! At the full sun!" But the moon
when it's full, with its intoxicating pull,
is a whole different story.

Tears cleanse your eyes.
So that you could see
what you couldn't before.

We cry at birth and in our early years to
express ourselves before we learn to speak.
Yet it still remains a part of us for the rest
of our lives. Because no matter how many
words we know, sometimes, what we feel
can only surface through our primordial
form of expression.

The hammer of life hits everyone on
the right spot, with the right chisel,
under the right pressure. Based on
what they're made of. To shape them
into what they're meant to be.

Warriors flaunt their scars
and the stories they hold.
Oh how I wish,
you wouldn't hide yours.

Many who suffer
cause others the same.

Many who burn
set others aflame.

But few remain
with no worldly gain

by being the light
for those in pain.

Sometimes replacing "*what's wrong?*"
with "*what was the best part of your day?*"
makes all the difference.

And I fought
until my heart was black and blue
because I thought
it was a fight worth having you
but I forgot
as I tried to make it through
that I cannot
have us without you trying too.

———————————————————

Those who are blinded by their own
wounds may inflict even greater pain
on others without ever realizing it.
Self-pity robs the heart of empathy.

The tragedy of great love
stories is that they're told
in the past tense.

———————————————

If only we'd part
ways like the sun.
That paints the sky
with every goodbye.
In shades of red and gold,
that fade away
into shades of grey.
A most fitting way to end,
like fire ends in ashes.

Behind every eulogy
is a burden of regret.
Of words unspoken
and love unexpressed.

———————————————————

The world is split
between those who feel too much
and those who barely feel at all.
And something tells me,
the latter went numb
being the former for too long.

I've missed you
before I even met you,
so how could I not
when you're not here.
I've loved you
before I even met you,
so how could I not
when you're everywhere.

"I wish I could forget it all"
"Forget what?" I asked.
And he stood there in silence,
staring into the distance...
Remembering it all over again.

In trying to forget, I remembered.
And brought back all the pieces of
a memory I had once dismembered.

———————————————

The downside to being able to
sense love from afar, is knowing
when it's being withdrawn.

———————————————

Sometimes life teaches us to be there
for ourselves by taking everyone else
away at a time when we need them the
most. *It's when all the other lights go
out, that you begin to notice your own.*

Like a wounded child
that runs to his mother.
Here I am, Lord, help me.
Heal me. I've hurt myself.

And the heart places doors
where the hurt builds its walls.

I can't imagine the brutal battles
you must have fought. For your
heart to be this soft. For your soul
to be so kind. And for the thought
of you, to be so comforting.

Time slowed down today
for a yellow leaf's ballet.
Separated from its branch.
Performing its final dance.
To subtle cello in the wind.

There's right, there's wrong.
And then there are blurred lines
in between where we slip and fall.

I haven't broken yet,
not quite,
but I might be on the brink.
With the stages of my heart
tonight,
as I'm in and out of sync.
Oh the pages you make me write,
my love,
I'm running out of ink.
My third eye could see you all
night,
and never dare to blink.

Turn your pain into art.
And if it heals one person,
then you've saved two lives.

Some people can sense
when a work of art
flows from a broken heart.
It's raw. It's pure.
Both the pain, and its cure.

I admire the sacred bond
of the sun and the moon.
But at times, even they
get in each other's way.
Where for a moment,
two radiant lamps
end up causing darkness.

There are memories that you think are
long gone and forgotten. But all it takes
is the right fragrance, the right breeze,
or the right place – and they come
rushing back from the dead.

For my rebellion and defiance,
you threw me to the lions,
not knowing they're my family.
With whom I sin and I pray,
and in the wilderness we slay
as we lust for our teeth
in the necks of our prey.
For blood is wine for a feast
when you're dining with beasts.

What makes you unforgettable
is not that I could talk to you, but
that I could sit with you in silence.

He turned towards the cheering crowd,
with eyes in search of his beloved's face.
Whose precious smile carried a value,
the world's applause could not replace.
Bleak is the victory
celebrated with strangers,
and sweet is a loss
in the arms of love.

It's often the most unwanted moments
that lead to the most desired ones.
And as a result, leaves us in a strange
place of being grateful for the worst
times of our lives.

Sometimes
bitter chapters
are *necessary*
for sweet ones
to follow.

SOLITUDE

I looked at the burgundy sky,
and saw a flock of birds fly by.
Oh it was a sight to see.
But then an eagle caught my eye.
Solitary. Poised. Wild and free.
The flock ain't for you, my friend.
Just as the crowd ain't for me.

If you're not comfortable
in your own company,
how could anyone else be?

I found myself alone. Lost.
Until I found myself, alone.

You are your oldest enemy and your oldest friend.
The longest relationship you'll ever have in this
world is with yourself. There isn't another soul that
knows you better than you do. And if a series of
events happen to leave you all alone, and lost, know
that *you're in the perfect place to find yourself*. To
discover who you really are. Past the layers of who
you thought you were, or should be, or who the world
expects you to be. Self discovery is the beginning of
finding your purpose in life.

At times I fear
if what I feel is even real.
Seems hard to tell apart
what is here,
from what has passed on.
In my solitude,
it all shines bright
like stars on a dark night.
But then, don't stars glow
even after they're long gone?

Our awareness decides our company.
We could be alone, and be with people.
Or be around people, and be alone.

So long as I stayed on my own path, towards my own
purpose, I remained detached yet lovingly embraced
all the souls I met along the way. Because my journey
was aligned with the truth: *that we are all solitary travelers
from birth to death on a temporary plane.* And any pain
I've experienced along the way was attaching my horse to
someone's who did not share the same journey as mine.
For even if they did, it would only be for a few miles. And
so I have strayed, hurt myself, and returned to my path
once more. With memories as scars to keep me from losing
my way again. As I head into the unknown, towards home.

Allow yourself to feel what you need
to feel when the moment calls for it.
Resisting what's endurable eventually
amounts to being unbearable.

We can spend a lifetime
getting to know others.
Yet make little to no effort
in knowing ourselves.
So we find it difficult being alone.
As our moments of solitude
are in the company of a stranger.

Fear of loneliness
beautifies bad company.

Maybe the real me isn't hiding
behind many masks. Maybe all
of me refuses to hide behind one.

When they let you in,
don't forget you're a guest.
And if you let them in,
remember that is *your* home.

I retreat into the light
of Your remembrance.
So that I may heal
my wounded soul.
And gain strength
to rise above my demons,
to go back
into the mayhem
once more.

Though it's rare, I'm pulled by certain
towards them. Familiar strangers if you will.
Where I think: *I must get to know them more.*
As if they were a puzzle I'm desperate to solve.
But then I think that perhaps, that is how they
were meant to be admired. From a distance,
for their complexity and mysterious design.
And were I to get too close,
I might just ruin the whole art of it all.

Of all the mysteries in the universe,
the Self remains the greatest one.
As both the enemy and the friend.
The question, and the answer.
But also the lie, as well as the truth.

I have long embraced that I feel things so
very deeply. Love, as if my heart would
burst. Sorrow, as many agonizing deaths.
Joy, as though the moon were in my arms
or the entire galaxy in my chest. And so I
know, that my immortal soul is far greater
than my mortal body. And perhaps, when
I have returned to my forgotten home, I'll
look back at this world and say *that* was
one helluva ride.

Looking above, we ask the most
important questions. And looking
within, we find all the right answers.

Where do I begin?
The heart would be a good start.
As the truth needs no revision,
and no alterations for it to be.
It lives, just as lies do not.
It is, all that flows from the heart.

"How do you feel?"
Grateful that I can feel.

Perhaps it's not words, but silence
that may unlock this chest of yours.

I don't know
of battles more fierce
or victories more sweet
than in my war within.

Sometimes calm is only a few
deep breaths away from chaos.

The outcomes of our inner battles
hardly ever rely on which side is
right or wrong, weak or strong,
because in the end, the side that
wins is often the one we shine
our light of awareness on.

I sometimes wonder if my suffering is a
punishment or a blessing. And then I ask
myself, if it has hardened my heart with
self pity, or softened it with empathy. If
it has made me arrogant, or humble. If it
has filled me with despair, or hope in my
Maker's mercy. If it has blurred my vision
with ignorance, or given me clarity through
divine wisdom. And in there, I find my answer.

The sad part is, we crave from others
what we refuse to give to ourselves.
And so, on the surface we cry out
"love me, care for me, be kind to me."
But on a deeper level, the one that
connects us all, we say *"don't."*

After the blame game
and silent self-reflection,
we come to realize
that we're often victims
of our own oppression.

There's a calm in the storm,
and music in its winds.

It's dark. And your shadow
is no longer behind you.
Instead, you are within it.
And you're forced to embrace
all that you don't want to face.
Until it loses all power over you.

- *Healing*

The world gives when you let go
and takes when you hold on.
Silently conveying the truth,
that it's not your eternal home,
but only your journey towards it.

Who we truly are is answered best
by our deeds behind closed doors.

Every breath is worth more
than the previous one, as
we draw nearer to our last.

Is life made up of moments, or
is every moment a life of its own.
Where some are lived to their fullest,
and others barely so. Many of us ask,
how long is a lifetime. But I wonder,
how many lifetimes I have truly lived.

———————————————

We are works of fiction in the minds
of those who think they know us. As
characters they have the ability to
create and manipulate as they see fit.
In stories that we play no part in.

A lion that hunts for
survival in the jungle
does not envy the one
being fed in a zoo.

Others might have accomplished
more, or less, when they were your
age. But having been someone's age
isn't the same as having been in their
shoes. And so, there goes comparison
out the window.

Though I have a deep affection
for those close to me. The only time
I value the most, is when I'm alone,
in my own company. That is when I'm
closest to my Maker, and my eternal home.

———————————————————

What's gained from observing
others, is lost by judging them.

———————————————————

The heart doesn't like
to argue with the mind.
It prefers to speak
when the other is silent.

Rain is white noise, until you tune
yourself into it and hear its music.
In every drop, on every surface.
Orchestrated from above.

———————————————

Strange how the bitterness
of coffee makes life sweet.

———————————————

You may know me by what I write.
I may know you by what you read.
And who knows,
we might just be on the same page.

It reached the tip of my tongue, but I
couldn't say it. The tips of my fingers,
but I couldn't write it. At times I am
deluded into thinking it eluded me.
But I know, that it's hidden in a prison
in the depths of my soul.
Waiting. Hoping.
For courage to set it free.

———————————————————

How perfectly human
it is to be imperfect.

———————————————————

All that I own, begins to own me
the moment its presence or absence
influences my state of being.

I am not the picture you have
painted in your mind of me.
No matter how beautiful, or
horrible it may be. They are
your colors, and your artistry.

When confidence isn't sustained,
arrogance quietly takes its place.

It takes a pure heart to absorb
wisdom. And constant purification
of the heart to retain it.

Pride and insecurities blur the
lens of empathy. It's hard to place
yourself in anyone else's shoes
if you can't leave your own.

Our branches may not touch,
but our roots unite us as one.

We are made aware of
the state of our hearts
by how we think of others.

If good things die
of inattention, then
the good news is,
so do the bad.

Perhaps the devil's first
mistake was comparison,
that led to his arrogance.

A snake can't be a lion
and a lion can't be a snake.
Yet man can be both.

There's something about late hours
of the night. All the masks are taken
off. And the true self is unveiled.

I can't remember the last time I saw
the full moon when I wasn't alone.
And how it made me feel like I wasn't.
I know, that it does things to me. Yet
for all its wonder, and my curious
nature, I find more joy in its mystery,
than in trying to solve it.

Guard your thoughts
like your life depends on it.
...because it does.

When we're unaware of broken relationships with ourselves, we're unconsciously driven to seek out love and validation outside of us in an attempt to fill our void. But no matter how hard we try, nothing can mend what only we have the power to. It's at this point that we must go within to discover what went wrong. *What self inflicted wound has resulted in a loss of self love?* To find that, to forgive that, and to heal by earning back our love is one of the most fulfilling journeys of solitude.

Where were you when you
needed yourself the most?
Live such, that you never
have to answer that you were
searching for someone else.

You can't please everyone.
And if you do, it would be at
the expense of your authenticity.

———————————————————

"Why do you journey alone?"

Because the world said
it wouldn't know me,
until I knew myself.
And wouldn't love me,
until I loved myself.
But then somewhere, within the
countless moments of solitude,
I found a love much greater
than the world could ever offer.

FAITH

I found it strange
yet perfectly balanced;
that I needed my wounds
to heal my faith,
and my faith
to heal my wounds.

When you have a hard time
finding God in times of ease,
he puts you through hard times
to find him with ease.

Knowing that
the chirping of birds
and the sound of thunder,
the *calm* and the *storm,*
derive from the same Source;
gives me all the proof I need
to turn to no one,
but *One.*

My plans may be written in sand,
but my faith is carved in stone.
What's mine before my life began,
waits for me in the unknown.

In between what is taken from me,
and what is given to me, I am defined
by how I choose to be. Beautiful Patience
is the equilibrium between loss and hope.

Here I am
where I'm meant to be.
Headed to where
I'm destined to be.
Living through all
that's best for me.
Said my heart
to the rest of me.

I don't pretend to know my fate. Nor am
I certain of what's written for me a minute
from now. But God knows I love gifts and
surprises. And that's enough to put my heart
at ease, knowing that my destiny is written
by the One who knows me and loves me
far more than I have the ability to.

I am at peace. Because I have surrendered
what I can't handle, to the One more than
capable of handling it. I am at ease.
Knowing that what is best for me, is
already destined for me. – Affirmations

Sometimes we say we've let go. That
we've surrendered. All the while having
our old plans tucked in our back pockets.
Hoping that life wouldn't notice.

———————————————————

Faith is the currency
we buy our dreams with.

———————————————————

Funny how we wait for our prayers to be
answered to strengthen our faith, when in
reality it's having strong faith that opens
our doors to what we ask for.

We suffocate when we raise others
to a place meant for God alone.
Flowers cannot replace the sun
with one of their own
and expect to survive.

God hears what others don't,
and listens when others won't.
Sees what others don't,
and cares when others won't.

Patience
is to admire the stars
as you await dawn.

Sometimes we're afraid of letting things
go their natural way because deep down,
we believe nature to always be slow.
The process of a seed into a tree is natural,
but so is lightning.
Letting things flow in their natural order,
in divine order, is not a matter of the length
of time, but the perfect time.

"And what caused you
to leave your past behind?"

I emptied the poison from my cup
so I may fill it with Your wine.

———————————————————

I planted the seeds of my sorrow
in this forgotten and barren land.
Watered with tears I couldn't swallow
and blood from my weary hands.
Oh the harvest that was to follow,
as roses from Arabian sands
tell tales of a better tomorrow,
and hope in my Maker's plans.

Blessings Multiply
when you're looking *at* them
and not for them.

Our response to days gone by
shape our days to come.

Hope does not enter the heart
where self-pity resides.

What's meant for you will be yours.
And what's not could never be. The
comfort of this statement is based on
your level of trust in God. Who gives
without measure. And takes only to
replace it with much better.

My faith is the evidence
and the answer to my prayer
before it's made manifest.

Life has a way
of filling all voids
worthy of our expectations.

DESIRE

They tell dreamers
to be realistic
when reality itself
is made up of dreams.

Painting pictures in the night sky
with the visions of my mind's eye
from a fire in me that set ablaze
a desire in me for better days.

Another night has gone by
without us having spoken.
And yet in silence, we did.

I paint your image
in places you can't see.
In empty spaces
around me,
and within me.
With my eyes open,
and closed.

It's sad, that we'd write
for the world to read,
what we're unable to say
to the one it's meant for.

———————————————

The only thing sadder than letters
written and never sent, are the ones
delivered but misread. And even worse,
is the writer swinging on a pendulum
between fear and hope. Between not
writing at all, and writing it all.

A part of me wants to be
in the depths of my reverie
until I substitute every
scarred and charred memory
with colors that wouldn't be
a heartbroken death of me.

There's something about
the colors of autumn,
quietude of winter,
rebirth in spring,
and radiance of summer,
that reminds me of you.

All that is finite cannot satisfy
the appetite of an eternal soul.
Only the Infinite can.

———————————————————

The great delusion is to assume we would be
happy if we get what we want. Perhaps for a
moment, yes. But it is impossible to cease
wanting more. *Desire* is part of our nature.
And without gratitude in the process, between
desires and their fulfillment, life becomes a
series of long miserable journeys with
short happy endings.

Assume me,
and I'll consume you.
For I appear when I am felt
and disappear when I am not.
I am all that is good,
and all that is not.

Strange is our notion of freedom.
For which children seek adulthood,
and adults, their inner child.

Imagine,
but with care.
For all your visions
are a form of prayer.

Daydreaming.
I could be all alone
in what I believe in.
In what I'm drawn to,
where I belong to,
and yet I'd still be
in the right company.

It's the strangest thing, how all the
events and people are drawn to us.
Pulled by the invisible strings of our
greatest fears, and our deepest desires.

I have no problem with falling asleep.
I just love my life too much to let go.
And I have no problem with waking up.
I just love my dreams too much to let go.
Perhaps my problem is love.
Or perhaps, it's letting go.

Being too attached isn't a sign of love, but
fear of loss. The ability to let go comes from
being confident that what's meant for you is
already yours. And doesn't need to be held so
tight, or even held at all. And all that leaves only
makes way for something far better to replace it.

How do I stop you from being the subject
of my mind chatter? By changing the course
of my inner conversations to your Maker.
Because in the end, all beauty of the creation
points towards the Creator.

Laughter in the streets
and tear drops in mansions,
redefines wealth.

Man is the only animal who
may confuse the thrill of the
hunt with love for his prey.

Would you listen, for once.
said the brain.

No, it won't hurt this time.
said the heart.

I think of all the prayers you answered
before I felt the need to make them. All
the wishes you fulfilled before I could
ever have them. I think of all the ways
you've taken care of me, for as long, and
even longer than I can remember. And as
I weigh it all against what my heart
desires today, I raise my hands to pray,
and all that leaves my lips is *thank you.*

Desire itself can get in the way of
getting what we desire, when it makes
us feel incomplete without having
what we want.

A dream held on to long enough
unfolds the way for it to manifest.

———————————————————

Strange how we sacrifice our
happiness to have things that
might make us happy.

———————————————————

Find me, said joy, between
your dreams and memories.

RISE

And if they ask
Who will help you rise,
say the King of kings
Who causes the sun to rise.

―――――――――――――――

I promise,
healing begins with the hurt.
And I promise,
that you'll never be the same.
But I can't promise,
if you'll rise a victor or a victim.
Though I can promise,
that *you*, have the freedom to choose.

Walking away is easier when
you weigh the pleasure of it all
against the misery that follows.

If a step away from them
is a step closer to you,
then keep walking.

It takes courage
to let people in.
And even more
to let them go.

And then there are those
who choose to smile
despite their chaos within.

Grateful in receiving.
Graceful in letting go.

First, you have to find someone
who would believe in you, even
if the whole world wouldn't.

Where? Look in the mirror.

It's not that you loved the wrong person, if it
wasn't reciprocated. It's not that you forgave
the wrong ones, if they hurt you again. We
can only give what we have. And sometimes,
you may have more than others to give. But
more importantly, what we give, *always finds
its way back to us multiplied*. So give, love
and forgive. As if they were seeds you'd plant
in your own paradise.

Broken and healed is far
stronger than having never
been broken at all. And the
stronger we are, the more
love we can contain.

The fear is not in letting go of the person you
thought was the one, but of all the fantasies you've
ever had of your future with them. The dismantling
of those visions, of letting beautiful dreams crumble
into a nightmare of the unknown; *therein lies the
true terror*. But also, *a new beginning*, a reunion
with your greater self once abandoned. A journey
that takes every ounce of bravery within you. But
an ascension worth every step you daringly take.

What is freedom? It's traveling light,
and letting go of everything that's only
meant to be a part of your journey.

What is peace? It's surrendering every
desire and worry to the One who keeps
the entire universe in order.

And love? It's our most natural state
of being when one is free and at peace.

Dear Traveler,
You carry too much of your past.
Let its lessons accompany you.
And forgiveness unburden you.

———————————————

And I am sorry
that you thought
my forgiveness
meant an open door.
When in fact
that was a lock
for which the key
exists no more.

———————————————

Life is short when
you walk with purpose.
And too long when
you aimlessly wander.

They may break your heart but never your
soul. You can't break the light. And when
you rise, and rise you shall like the morning
sun in all its glory, your vengeance would
not be to imitate those who wronged you.
But to cast your rays upon the world from
all that burns you. And say *this*, is how I
turn my pain into growth, hate into love,
anger into mercy, and my grief into grace.

There are days when my greatest triumphs are
in having done nothing more than courageously
chosen to *live*. For I have not chosen a partial life,
but a life in its fullness. For its darkest nights, and
brightest days. For God's mysterious ways. For its
colors and grays. For today's sorrows and better
tomorrows. For its warmth and its chills. For its fire
and ice. For the poetry my heart spills. For both its
hell and paradise. So let the great waves of life flow
through me, without resistance. And let them see, that
the only one I bow down to, is *unimaginably greater*.

Is it their absence
that causes your inner void,
or your inner void
that causes them to leave.
And is it their presence
that sparks your self-love,
or your self-love
that welcomes them in.

———————————————————

It's not your love for them, but
the lack of it for yourself, that gives
anyone power over how you feel.
An imbalance caused by energetically
feeding someone more than yourself.

Do not despair
over a minor mistake
that life took as payment
for a greater lesson.

———————————————

You don't realize how much you've healed,
until you begin to notice a sense of relief in
parts of you where tension and pain went on
for years unnoticed. A sort of numbness that
crept in somewhere along the way to protect
you. A cocoon, from which you can feel
yourself slowly and gracefully, rising anew.

I'm comfortable with wearing my heart
on my sleeve. It isn't a fragile thing to be
locked away. Transparent as it may be, it
isn't made of glass that could crack and
shatter beyond repair. On the contrary,
my heart has been tested and proven to
be the strongest part of me I know.

Kings and Queens
feel the weight
of the crown
long before
they wear it.

Compliments are
medicine for the spirit.
The right dosage cures,
and overdose kills.

―――――――――――――――

The venom of an unforgiven past
may poison the unrelated present.

―――――――――――――――

It was what it was and it's gone.
It is what it is and it's going.
It only hurts when you try to hold on.
So let go, and you'll keep on growing.

For every place you're meant to go,
there's a place you're meant to leave.
For every breath you must take, there's
one you must let go. And so, letting go
is never a loss. But a clearing to allow
more of life to happen through you.

She said hello like the sunrise
and goodbye like the sunset.
Loved like the full moon
and let go like the sky wept.

Who would've thought
that some day
we would be chapters
in each other's books.
But the story must go on
for as long as I breathe.
And these pages must turn
through my joy and my grief.

It's alright if they forget
what you've done for them.
As long as you don't forget
that you never did it
for them to remember.

In forgiving you, I am forgiven.
In giving you, I am given.
In loving you, I am loved.
And in praying for you, I prosper.

Forgiveness is a process. And if the pain is
deep, you may have to forgive more than a few
times for the same wound. And that's alright.
Because every time you forgive, you heal a
little more than before. Until one day, you look
back and instead of pain, all you feel is relief.

How can we taste the sweetness
of paradise here, if our hearts are
filled with what's forbidden there.

Observe the behavior of children
and absorb the wisdom of elders.
They are both great teachers of life.

My calm composure
is not the absence of chaos,
but my dominion over it.

We fall in love
with the creation,
and rise in love
with the Creator.

My mind searches for reasons to justify how I feel.
So if I'm hurt or angry, all things unforgiven or once
thought to have been forgiven arise to further fuel my
state. And if I am happy and content, my mind finds
reasons to make sense of it all as well. But somewhere
in between the way I think and feel, lies my power;
my ability to choose the direction of my thoughts,
and decide how I feel. From this, I know that my life
is as good or as bad, as I want it to be.

Letting go is an emotional process,
not an intellectual one. If you've
felt your way into a situation, you
can't overthink your way out of it.
The only way to leave is through
the same door you went in.

———————————————

Life is a journey best traveled light. And that
can be challenging if love and attachment are
entwined. There's so much to love in this world,
yet nothing to take from here. But once we see
the difference between the two and keep them
apart, we can go on loving joyously and tirelessly,
as is in our nature, until our very last breath.

Looking back,
what I once complained of,
I now thank for.
What I once ran away from,
I now embrace.

Never chase anyone at
the cost of losing yourself.
There's not a soul worth
the price of yours.

I'll let you in,
if you leave your
mask at the door.

I am the river.
I am the sea.
I am beyond
all that I can see.
I am the valley.
I am the mountain.
I am as low, and
as high as I can be.

Do you see the similarity
between sunrise and sunset.
Between *rise* and *fall.*

There's beauty in both,
if you're willing to look.

A Bedtime Story

Once upon a time in a land far far away,
there lived a raging fire,
who was unhappy every day.
Always alone, without any friends.
Burning everything he touches,
though it's not what he intends.
Tired and frustrated of his loneliness,
he asked his Maker to remove his stress.
Just then he heard water speak from the sea:
 "If you're searching for freedom,
  I am your only key"
But as he walked towards water from the dry land,
out gushed a stream of oil
from underneath the sand.
 "I'll make you better and stronger,
  if you would take my hand"
Said oil to fire in a believable voice.
And fire thought, this must be the right choice!
Though from the shore, water called once more
 "Fire oh fire, it's me whom you should desire"
But he took the hand of oil,
and ignored the voice of water.
And he began to feel stronger, even hotter.
With more flames than he could ever have thought of.
I guess he finally had something he could be proud of.

So he headed back to the forest,
with his head held high and chest out.
Yet burning everything he touched
got him all stressed out.
He had turned to ashes
all the grass and the trees.
Killing all that he loved,
as if he were a disease.
Realizing the deception of oil,
oh what a grievous mistake.
He finally saw water as his only escape.
So he made his way back
towards the crystalline sea.
That had once claimed to be
his freedom's key.
Full of guilt and shame
from his ignorant actions.
He felt both comfort and pain
with water's interaction.
Perhaps fate had decided
the two opposite's attraction.
And so with every touch,
fire would lose a flame.
Until an unchained and free smoke
is all he became.
Rising his way up to the heavens
away from the sea.
And the once imprisoned fire,
was finally free.

LOVE

It's in the squeeze of a hug.
As two hearts in love try to touch.
Past the prison of skin and bones.
It's in every inch of space between
distanced bodies, with intimate souls.
Together, apart. Together in thought.

Words are meant to reveal
what we think and what we feel.
But a comfortable silence between
two in love, might reveal far
more than the words they know.

The Arabic word for Human is *Insaan*.
Which branches from "one who forgets"
and "one who loves." And so, it makes
one think, is it one who forgets to love?
or one who forgets to love the One who
gave him the ability to love.

Loving never hurts, but asking for it
does. And I think that's where we often
get it wrong, when we find ourselves in
what we seem to think is love, yet feel the
opposite of what it should really feel like.

When you see the world
through purity of love, it
glances back with a smile.

———————————————————

Does "I love you" mean "I want you,"
or "I want you to be happy." Because
sometimes they're the same thing. But
sometimes, they're not. And that's when
we're faced with one of the most difficult
choices in life, in how we define love.

You can love birds without caging
them and flowers without plucking
them. Love thrives without the bondage
of possession and expectations.

The moon glows different
when you express your love for it.

Will you not admire
the flawless work
of your Maker
by loving yourself?

What makes someone a soulmate? Is it
an inexplicable familiarity with another
soul? If so, then every poet and artist
whose work pulls me into a world that
feels like home, is my soulmate.

When I feel my heart stray from its true
purpose, I remind it that I choose love. And
if it responds by recalling the necessary evil
that lives in all of us, some more than others,
I then remind it that *I choose to love the
good that exists in everyone*. And that seems
to put a peaceful end to my inner conflict.

I wonder how much of the sunset's attraction lies in its fleeting nature. As I can only stare at its picture for a few seconds at most. But being there, in the midst of its burgundy and gold, I can't leave until it's dark. Perhaps sunsets aren't so different from those we love.

"...But why her?"

She's the perfect balance
of dreams and nightmares.

Some fall for the Soul.
Others for its garment.
Only one is eternal.

I am a prisoner of a love that sets me free.
That makes me weak in the knees and lifts
me up at the same time. A place where I am
lost, and found. Heard, without making a sound.
Where I am myself, or rather who I choose to be.
Present, without a trace of who I used to be.

Maybe our pursuit of perfection in
everything we love, and love itself,
is the soul's innate desire to seek the
One it came from.

If I am to love you in ways
that sets you ablaze
and turns nights into days,
how could I promise
not to ever hurt you?

You think you have
love all figured out until
it demands a sacrifice.

The thought of your face
puts a smile on mine.
And when you rise like the sun
the other stars don't shine.

I know, that there are parts of you
I'll never know. So I admire the
scattered pieces of your puzzle
as abstract art.

———————————————————

Show me your flaws, and I'll tell
you why they make you beautiful.
And that smile could stop wars,
or perhaps, even cause them.

———————————————————

There are givers,
and takers.
Rich, and poor.
Not in wealth,
but in love.

You can love even the most seemingly
unlovable people, if you free them of
your judgement. And see them as
merely a channel at any given moment,
a potential for both good and evil, in all
their varying degrees.

Many kings saw your walls
and laid siege to claim you.
But not a brick of it falls
for those who aim to tame you.

And when my world within loses light,
I am visited by vivid memories
of the many souls I love.
Surrounding me, soothing me,
in the shape of fireflies,
amidst the dark forest of my thoughts.

I shall love you until the end of days,
immeasurably, but with my self-respect
intact. For if I sacrifice that, then I would
lose love for myself, and with it, my will
to love others the way I am designed to.

As for those we love,
what separates warmth,
from a burn, and a shiver;
is the right distance.

All that glitters in the night sky
would lose its value at arm's length.
You on the other hand,
are a star from afar,
and a diamond up close.

I don't believe in love at first sight.
But I do believe in the reunion of souls,
that have met before in another life.
In a place outside of time and space.

- Soulmates

It's not merely being loyal
but where your loyalties lie.
For even a lie asks
you to stay true to it.

Some people become more beautiful
as you get to know them. The light of
good character has a way of radiating
through the body.

Love was here long before time
and space. And so it transcends
all external separation.

No matter how much you're loved,
to *feel loved*, you must be seen for
who you really are. That's when every
ounce of love given, is a pound felt.

A moment for some,
and a lifetime for many.
Such is the journey
from the heart
to the tongue.

I swim in your love
but drown in your Maker's.

Everyone is as beautiful
as you want them to be.
Their moon reflects
the light of *your* sun.

Bit by bit, love within me
grew, until I was in love.

A mother's love is the reason why
amidst deafening cries and gunfire,
the wounded soldier in the trench
can only hear her lullaby.

Those you love are a part of you,
even if they're far apart from you.
And those you don't, are invisible
as ghosts, even if they're close.

When the tongue fails to convey
what the heart has in store,
Silence
becomes the language of love.

I love you. And perhaps that
would mean more after my time
has come. Since words of the dead
seem to have more life than those
uttered by the living.

I tell the moon about you,
from time to time.
Hoping that even a crescent
glows for you like it's full.

———————————————

Odd, but true. My heart
beats faster at the thought
of you. Changing its rhythm
to your name from mine.
To three syllables from two.

To every soul that I love,
to the wild and free.
To those close to me,
and those closer, in memory.
To the living, and the dead.
To those taking their first steps,
and those breathing their last breaths..
My love for you, will outlive this life.

From the moon to the sun
the bright serpent flows.
Through the seat of the soul
where the emerald glows.
In love, my spirit takes flight.
To reunite with light upon light.

For more poetry and prose visit

Instagram: @suhaib.rumi

Twitter and Fb: @BySuhaibRumi

Made in the USA
Las Vegas, NV
13 February 2023

67404134R00080